Let's Explore

DENMARK

FILLED WITH PLENTY OF FACTS, PHOTOS AND FUN TO LEARN ABOUT DENMARK

RACHEL MORTIMER

CONTENTS

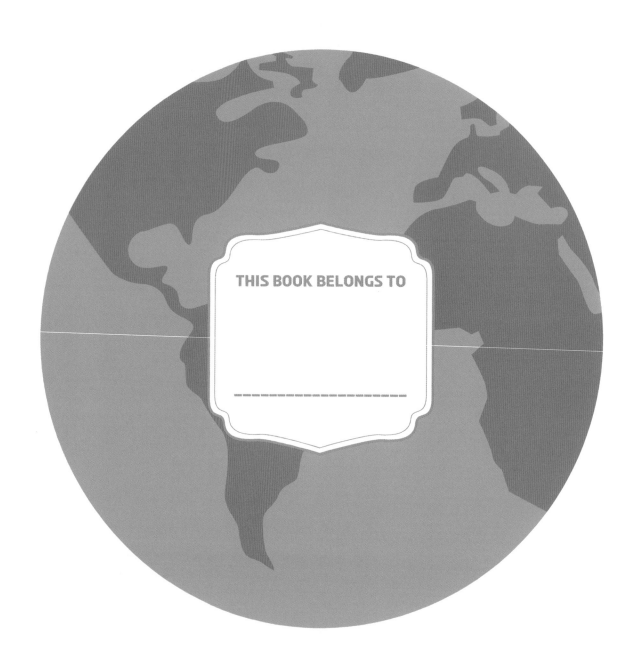

THIS BOOK BELONGS TO

Welcome To Denmark

Welcome to Denmark, a captivating country nestled in Northern Europe, renowned for its picturesque landscapes, warm-hearted people, and captivating past! Did you know that Denmark is often referred to as the "Land of Fairy Tales" due to its rich folklore and enchanting landscapes? In this book, you will delve into the intriguing history, vibrant culture, and remarkable landmarks of this extraordinary nation. Prepare yourself for an exhilarating journey through the wonders of Denmark, where every page unveils a new adventure!

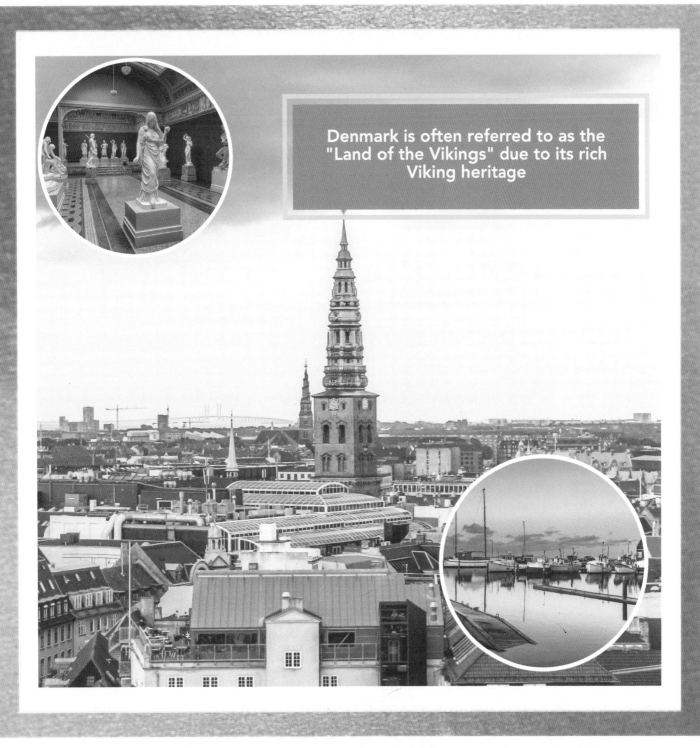

Denmark is often referred to as the "Land of the Vikings" due to its rich Viking heritage

Map

Denmark is a country adorned with stunning green landscapes, rolling hills, and picturesque coastlines. When you look at the map of Denmark, you'll notice its location in the northern part of Europe, bordered by the North Sea and the Baltic Sea. The country is divided into several regions, including Jutland, Zealand, Funen, and many more, each offering their own unique charm and attractions. Get ready to embark on a captivating journey through this extraordinary country and uncover the treasures that await in every corner!

Capital

The capital of Denmark is called Copenhagen, and it is a vibrant and lively city! Did you know that Copenhagen has a history dating back over 1,000 years? This means that it has been home to many people and witnessed centuries of fascinating stories. There are countless exciting things to explore and experience in Copenhagen. You can visit the iconic Christiansborg Palace, which has served as the residence of Danish royalty, or take a leisurely stroll along the picturesque Nyhavn Harbor. Don't forget to indulge in delicious Danish cuisine, such as smørrebrød (open-faced sandwiches) and traditional pastries like wienerbrød.

Rosenborg Castle, located in Copenhagen, Denmark, is a majestic fortress with a rich history and enchanting beauty. Built in the early 17th century, the castle is surrounded by lush gardens and serves as a remarkable testimony to Danish architectural grandeur.

Flag

The flag of Denmark is a unique and significant emblem. It consists of a solid red field with a white Scandinavian cross that extends to the edges of the flag. The cross represents Christianity and reflects Denmark's historical ties to the Danish Church. The design of the flag dates back to the 13th century and has since become a cherished symbol of Danish identity and unity. When you see the Danish flag proudly waving in the wind, it represents the rich history, values, and spirit of the Danish people.

Language

In Denmark, the official language spoken by the majority of the population is Danish. Danish is a North Germanic language and is closely related to Norwegian and Swedish. It has its own unique alphabet and pronunciation. While Danish is the primary language, many Danes also speak English fluently, especially in urban areas and among the younger generation. Being multilingual is highly valued in Denmark, and learning English is a common part of the education system. So, when you visit Denmark, don't be surprised to hear the melodious sounds of Danish, and you might even have the opportunity to practice your English skills too!

1.   Hello - Hej (pronounced "hi")
2.   Goodbye - Farvel (pronounced "far-vel")
3.   Thank you - Tak (pronounced "tahk")
4. Please - Vær så venlig (pronounced "ver soh ven-lee")
5. Excuse me - Undskyld (pronounced "oons-kool")

Food

The cuisine of Denmark is a delightful fusion of traditional Danish recipes and modern international influences. Danish cuisine is known for its emphasis on fresh, seasonal ingredients and simple yet flavourful preparations. Smørrebrød, open-faced sandwiches piled high with a variety of toppings like pickled herring, smoked salmon, or roast beef, are a quintessential Danish specialty. You can also indulge in delicious Danish pastries, known as wienerbrød, which come in various flavors like cinnamon, almond, or custard-filled. Another popular Danish dish is frikadeller, savory meatballs served with potatoes and gravy. And let's not forget about the mouthwatering Danish cheeses and delectable seafood, such as smoked salmon and fresh herrings. Danish cuisine is a true treat for your taste buds, and you'll find plenty of delicious options to satisfy your cravings during your culinary journey in Denmark.

Smorrebrod

Biksemad

Stjerneskud

Wildlife

Denmark is home to a diverse range of wildlife, both on land and in the surrounding waters. One of the most iconic animals you might encounter is the red deer, which roams freely in Denmark's forests. The country is also known for its population of Danish spotted pigs, known for their distinctive spots and flavorful meat. If you visit the coastal areas, you might be lucky enough to spot seals basking on the rocks or swimming in the sea.

Denmark's waters are teeming with marine life, including various species of fish, such as cod, herring, and plaice. Keep your eyes peeled for playful harbor porpoises, the smallest marine mammals found in Danish waters. Denmark's natural landscapes provide a habitat for many bird species, including the majestic white-tailed eagle, the graceful swan, and the colorful kingfisher.

Denmark is home to many animals such as bears, deer, foxes, badgers, otters, and various species of birds.

Landmarks

Denmark is home to a rich tapestry of historic and cultural landmarks that are sure to captivate visitors. One notable landmark is the iconic Kronborg Castle, located in Helsingør. This majestic Renaissance fortress is famously known as the setting for Shakespeare's play "Hamlet."

For a glimpse into Denmark's royal heritage, a visit to Amalienborg Palace is a must. This elegant palace complex serves as the official residence of the Danish royal family. If you're interested in Viking history, make sure to explore the ancient ruins of Jelling, a UNESCO World Heritage site that features impressive Viking-era burial mounds and rune stones. Denmark is also home to the iconic Little Mermaid statue, inspired by Hans Christian Andersen's fairy tale. Situated along the waterfront in Copenhagen, this small but beloved statue is a symbol of Danish culture and attracts millions of visitors each year.

Frederiksborg Castle

Kronborg Castle, also known as Hamlet's Castle, is a magnificent Renaissance fortress located in Helsingør, Denmark. This UNESCO World Heritage Site is steeped in history and is famous for its association with William Shakespeare's play, "Hamlet."

Culture

The people of Denmark have a rich and vibrant culture that they hold dear to their hearts. Danish music is diverse and encompasses a wide range of genres, from traditional folk songs to contemporary pop and rock. Instruments like the accordion, violin, and guitar are commonly used in Danish music. Danish people also have a strong passion for sports, with football (soccer) being particularly popular. They gather to support their favorite teams and engage in friendly rivalries. Denmark is also renowned for its exceptional design and craftsmanship. Danish designers are known for their innovative and functional creations in areas such as furniture, fashion, and architecture.

Danish culture is known for its emphasis on hygge, a cozy and warm atmosphere that promotes comfort and togetherness. It also celebrates a strong sense of community, egalitarianism, and a love for nature, which is reflected in the Danes' passion for outdoor activities and sustainable living.

Weather

Denmark has a temperate maritime climate, characterized by mild and changeable weather patterns. The country experiences cool summers and mild winters, with temperatures varying depending on the season. It's advisable to be prepared for sudden weather changes, as rain showers can occur throughout the year. So, packing an umbrella or a raincoat is always a good idea when exploring Denmark.

Aalholm Castle, located on the island of Lolland in Denmark, is a magnificent historic castle that showcases the country's rich architectural heritage.

Glossary

- Denmark: A country situated in Europe, renowned for its captivating landscapes and captivating past.

- Copenhagen: The capital city of Denmark, where you can encounter numerous iconic landmarks and delve into Danish history and culture.

- Danish language: The official language of Denmark, spoken by the majority of the population.

- Danish flag: A flag featuring a bright red background with a white Scandinavian cross, symbolizing Danish heritage and national pride.

- Danish cuisine: Delectable dishes and treats that are beloved in Denmark.

Keep Learning

Congratulations on finishing this book about Denmark! You've learned so much about this fascinating country, but there's still so much more to discover and explore. Remember, learning doesn't have to stop when you finish a book or a lesson. There's always more to learn, discover, and explore.

Every time you learn something new, you expand your mind and your world. You become more curious, creative, and confident. So keep asking questions, trying new things, and exploring the world around you. Whether it's Denmark, or another country, or a subject that interests you, there's always something new to discover and learn. So keep learning and exploring, and see where your curiosity takes you!

Printed in Great Britain
by Amazon

36172849R00016